Discovering
TUTANKHAMUN'S
TOMB

Contents

Written by Juliet Kerrigan

 Collins

Who were the Ancient Egyptians?

In Egypt 7,000 years ago, people lived on
the banks of the longest river in the world – the Nile.
They called themselves "People of the Black Land"
because when the river flooded every year, it left
behind black mud and clay called silt.

The banks of the Nile were a good place to live.
Farmers grew wheat for making bread, barley for
making beer, and a plant called flax, used
to make clothes. Plants growing on
the river banks were made
into **papyrus** for writing on.
River mud was shaped into
bricks for building.
People travelled in boats along
the Nile, and caught fish
and birds.

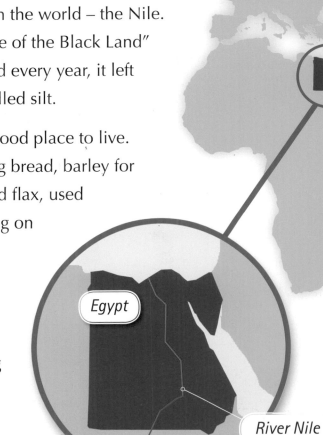

Egypt

River Nile

Over 5,000 years ago there were three **kingdoms** on the banks of the Nile. But in about 2950 BCE, the three kingdoms were joined together under one ruler called Narmer. Narmer, and all the kings who ruled after him, **worshipped** the gods, made sure people obeyed the law and led the army. They also put up statues and built palaces, temples and tombs.

Today, the People of the Black Land are known to us as the Ancient Egyptians.

FACT

On both sides of the river Nile, there were deserts, called the Red Land. These deserts were very hot and very dry. It would have been difficult to cross them, so the people who lived on the banks of the Nile were safe from attack by enemies.

Why did the Ancient Egyptians mummify bodies?

Ancient Egyptians believed that when they died they would enjoy an "afterlife" like the one they had left behind. They would eat and drink, play games and work in the fields. To take part in this afterlife, the body needed to be **preserved** by turning it into a mummy.

First, **embalmers** carefully removed the brain through the nose. Then, they took out most of the **internal organ**s through a slit in the side of the body. This was done because the organs rotted if they were left inside the body. However, Ancient Egyptians believed the dead person would still need them, so they were saved. The organs were put in special containers called canopic jars.

painted wooden canopic jars

After this, the body was covered in salt for 40 days to preserve it. It was then wrapped in linen bandages. Finally, the whole body was wrapped in a single sheet, and placed in a coffin. It was the **custom** to pour special oils over the body before the coffin lid was put on.

embalmers making a mummy by wrapping a preserved body in bandages

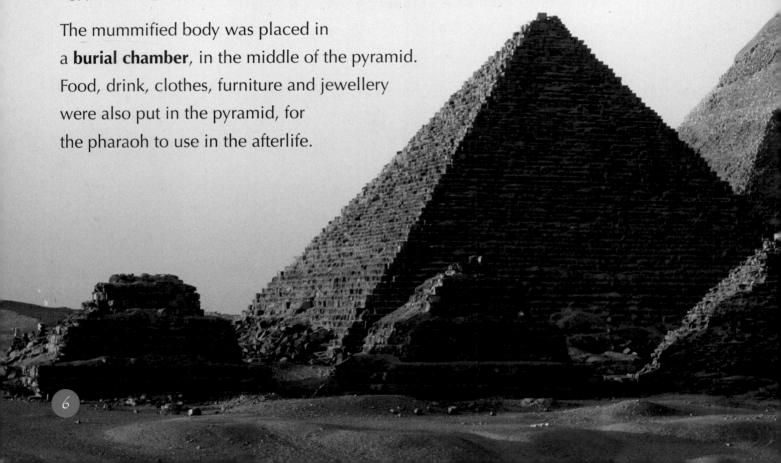

Why did the Ancient Egyptians build tombs?

Poor people were buried in simple graves in the sand. Rich and important people, like **nobles** or priests, were buried in small tombs. Egyptian kings, called pharaohs, built large stone tombs called **pyramids**.

The mummified body was placed in a **burial chamber**, in the middle of the pyramid. Food, drink, clothes, furniture and jewellery were also put in the pyramid, for the pharaoh to use in the afterlife.

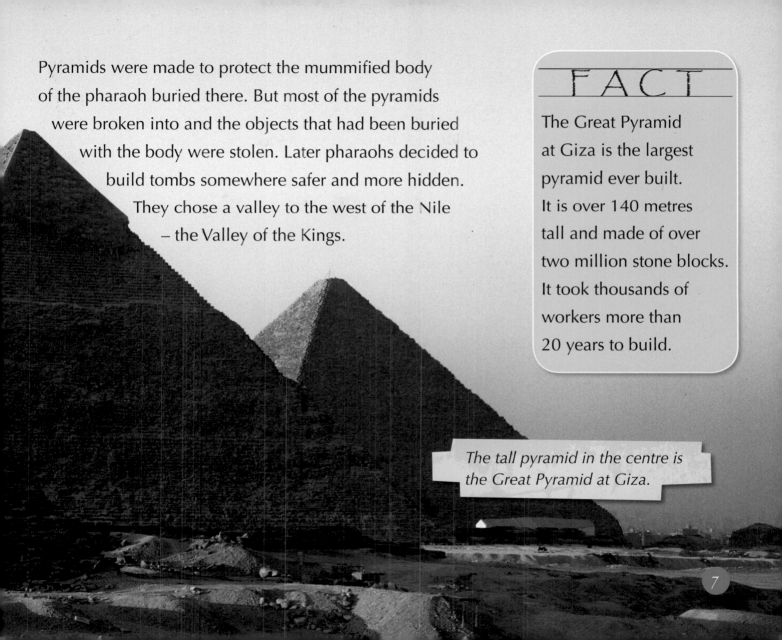

Pyramids were made to protect the mummified body of the pharaoh buried there. But most of the pyramids were broken into and the objects that had been buried with the body were stolen. Later pharaohs decided to build tombs somewhere safer and more hidden. They chose a valley to the west of the Nile – the Valley of the Kings.

FACT

The Great Pyramid at Giza is the largest pyramid ever built. It is over 140 metres tall and made of over two million stone blocks. It took thousands of workers more than 20 years to build.

The tall pyramid in the centre is the Great Pyramid at Giza.

What has been found in the Valley of the Kings?

Before 1922, **archaeologists** had discovered 61 tombs in the Valley of the Kings. They had been built from 1539 to 1069 BCE and they were very different from the pyramids. The tombs had been dug high up in the rock face to hide them.

The largest tomb had 121 rooms and corridors. Experts believe that it may have been made for the children of a pharaoh called Rameses II. Some of the tombs had painted walls and ceilings. A few had stone coffins with mummified bodies in them. But most of the tombs were empty.

tomb entrances in the Valley of the Kings

Only one tomb, discovered in 1905, gave a clue about how magnificent a royal burial might be. In it were two well-preserved mummies with **gilded** masks.
Chairs, beds and a jewellery box were found, but robbers had stolen the jewels.

The tombs in the Valley of the Kings were no safer than the pyramids had been.

the mask of Yuya

the mask of Tuya

Who was Tutankhamun?

In 1907, a wooden box was found buried in the Valley of the Kings. Written on it in Ancient Egyptian writing, called hieroglyphs, was the name "Tutankhamun".

Experts knew that Tutankhamun was a pharaoh who ruled Egypt over 3,000 years before. He became pharaoh when he was eight or nine years old and he ruled for ten years, from 1333 to 1322 BCE. As he was so young, Tutankhamun would have had advisers who helped him to rule. Tutankhamun lived in the city of Akhetaten and later in Thebes and Memphis. He was married to a young girl called Ankhesenamun.

These hieroglyphs say:
"Tutankhamun, ruler of Heliopolis".

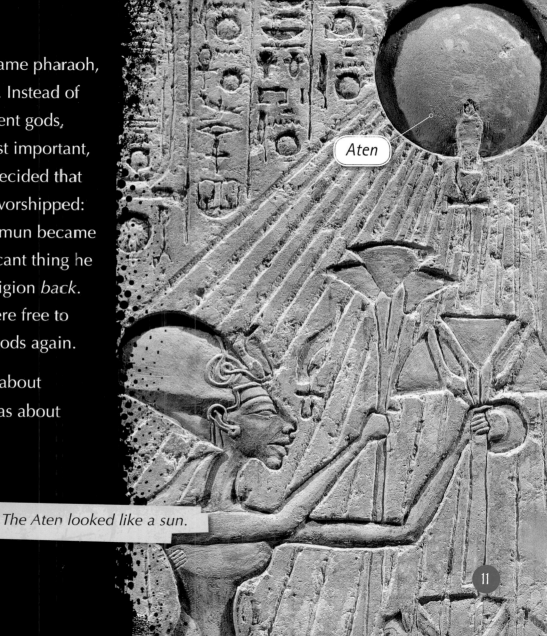

Before Tutankhamun became pharaoh, the religion had changed. Instead of worshipping lots of different gods, where Amun was the most important, the pharaoh at the time decided that only one god should be worshipped: the Aten. When Tutankhamun became pharaoh, the most significant thing he did was to change the religion *back*. The Ancient Egyptians were free to worship lots of different gods again.

Nothing else was known about Tutankhamun. But that was about to change.

Aten

The Aten looked like a sun.

How was Tutankhamun's tomb discovered?

Howard Carter had become interested in Egypt when he was 17 years old and he got a job drawing objects that had been dug up by archaeologists. He also drew plans of tombs and temples. He learnt how to excavate from archaeologists who were famous at that time: Gaston Maspero and Flinders Petrie. In 1899, Carter had found six royal tombs at Thebes (today called Luxor) in Egypt and in 1907 he worked for Lord Carnarvon, organising his excavations in Egypt.

Flinders Petrie excavated many important sites in Egypt.

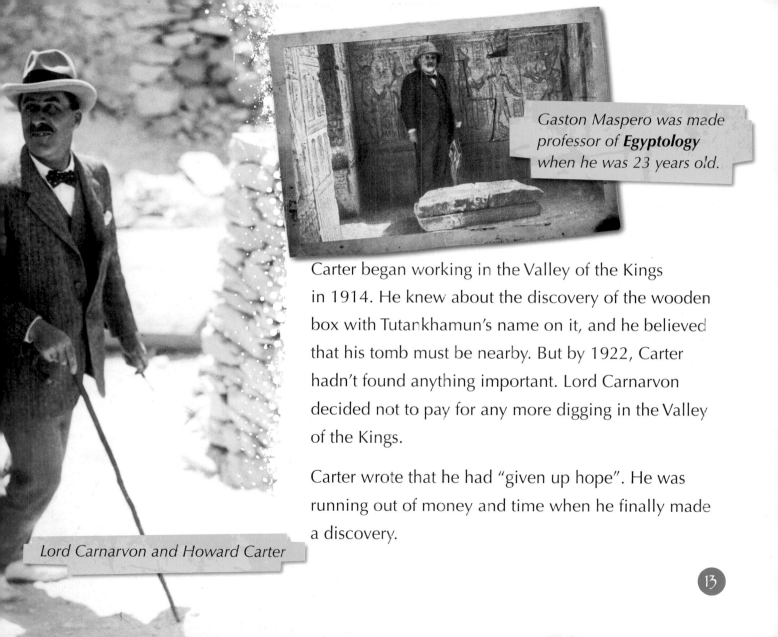

Carter began working in the Valley of the Kings in 1914. He knew about the discovery of the wooden box with Tutankhamun's name on it, and he believed that his tomb must be nearby. But by 1922, Carter hadn't found anything important. Lord Carnarvon decided not to pay for any more digging in the Valley of the Kings.

Carter wrote that he had "given up hope". He was running out of money and time when he finally made a discovery.

Lord Carnarvon and Howard Carter

On 4 November 1922, Carter was working on another tomb, when he found a step in the sand. It led *underneath* the tomb he was working on. By 20 November, Carter and his team had uncovered 16 steps leading down to a blocked doorway. On the doorway was a name in hieroglyphs. It was the name Carter had been looking for: Tutankhamun.

Howard Carter and the Egyptian workers in the tomb

When he dug down, Carter found a tunnel in the rock. It was full of stones and rubble and it led to another blocked doorway. When he made a small hole in that doorway he saw models of animals, statues of people, furniture and the glint of gold. At last, Carter had found the tomb of Tutankhamun.

the view of the first room that Carter saw

What was in Tutankhamun's tomb?

When Carter broke through the doorway and entered the tomb, he found four small rooms. Carter gave each of the four rooms a name: the antechamber, the annexe, the treasury and the burial chamber.

antechamber

annexe

entrance

In each room treasures were piled high, but they were in a complete mess.
Carter realised that the tomb must have been robbed many years before. In his diary he
wrote that he could even see the fingerprints of the robbers on some of the jars of oil.

But unlike the other tombs in the Valley of the Kings, the robbers had
not taken everything. Carter knew immediately that he had
found something important. He wrote in a letter:
"Never before … had such an amazing sight
been seen."

burial chamber

treasury

The antechamber

The antechamber was the first room Carter found. In it there were beds, chests, chairs, vases and chariots, heaped in untidy piles. All the large objects had the name "Tutankhamun" written on them in hieroglyphs.

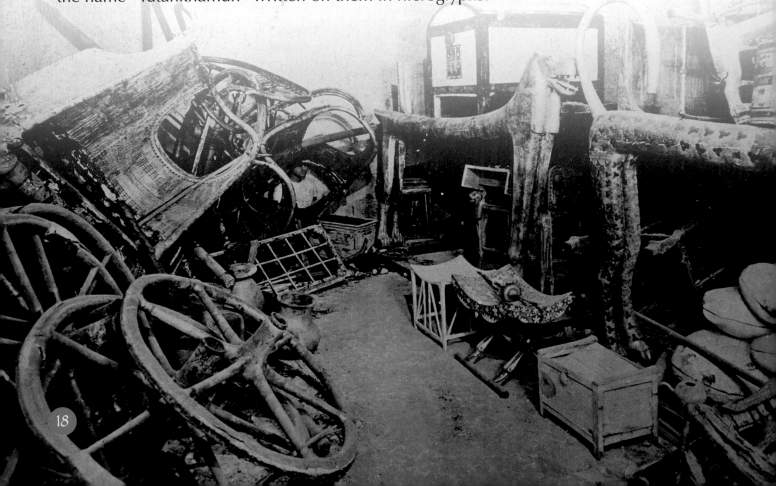

One of the first things Carter saw was a bed with two cows' heads and bodies. Each cow had a sun between its horns. The bed was made of wood, and covered in gold.

There were other beds in the tomb, which had been used. But experts don't think this bed was used in everyday life. It may have been made to take the pharaoh to the next world after he died – to take him to the afterlife.

The cow bed was meant to carry the pharaoh to the afterlife.

A wooden throne was also found in the antechamber. It was covered in gold and decorated with lions' heads and serpents with wings. Experts believe that Tutankhamun would have used this throne when he was alive.

There is an image of the sun on the back of the throne and the rays of the sun end in human hands. This image represents the most important god in Ancient Egypt when Tutankhamun was a child, the Aten. Experts believe that some of the hieroglyphs on the throne were changed when Tutankhamun changed the religion, and the sign for Aten was changed to the sign for the god Amun. The throne is important because it shows two different religious beliefs: the Aten and Amun.

In the picture, the pharaoh is sitting down. His wife is standing in front of him, putting oil on his shoulder. Both figures are wearing silver robes, elaborate head dresses, necklaces and bracelets. So the throne is also important because it shows the kind of clothing pharaohs wore, and it's one of the few images of Tutankhamun's wife.

For hundreds of years the style of Ancient Egyptian art had not changed. People were always drawn and painted in the same way. The image on the throne shows people in a new way; the pharaoh and his wife are shown relaxing, not posed in a formal way.

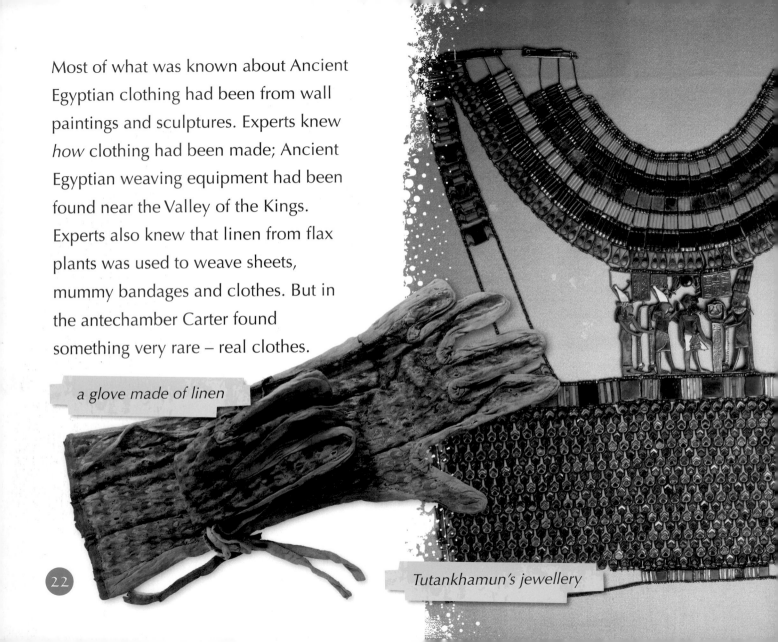

Most of what was known about Ancient Egyptian clothing had been from wall paintings and sculptures. Experts knew *how* clothing had been made; Ancient Egyptian weaving equipment had been found near the Valley of the Kings. Experts also knew that linen from flax plants was used to weave sheets, mummy bandages and clothes. But in the antechamber Carter found something very rare – real clothes.

a glove made of linen

Tutankhamun's jewellery

Ordinary Ancient Egyptians went barefoot, but not kings. In the tomb there were over 30 pairs of sandals and slippers. They were made of leather and papyrus and decorated with beads and gold. A robe decorated with gold sequins was discovered, and another with over 3,000 gold **rosettes** and linen with gold thread. From these finds we now know what clothes for the rich looked like, how they were made and decorated, and what they were made from. They also show that weavers were very **skilled** at this time.

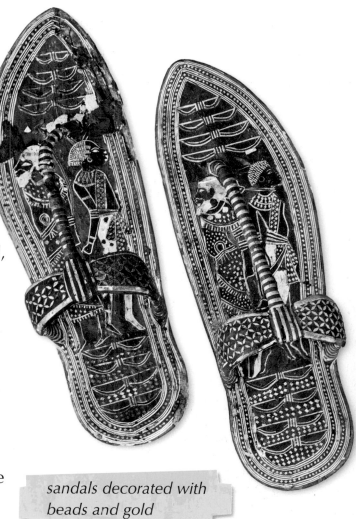

sandals decorated with beads and gold

The annexe

The room behind the antechamber looked like a storeroom. In it there were over 100 woven baskets filled with food such as dates, pomegranates, nuts and seeds, berries and garlic bulbs. About 12 loaves of bread were also found and a jar of honey labelled "good quality"! Wooden cases were filled with meat and 36 wine jars, now empty, were also in the annexe. Food and drink was left in the tomb for Tutankhamun to enjoy in the afterlife.

boxes of prepared food left in the tomb for Tutankhamun

a basket of fruit

From these finds we know what kind of food and drink was available at the time in Ancient Egypt, and what food rich people ate. The meat would have been considered a luxury item for the poor, who lived on bread and vegetables. But anyone, rich or poor, would have damaged their teeth eating some of the food.

The bread found in the tomb had desert sand and grit inside it. Experts believe that it blew in from the desert, and got into the flour from the grinding stones.

Ancient Egyptians used chests instead of cupboards in which to store things. In Tutankhamun's tomb, there were several chests with clothes and shoes in them. Rich Ancient Egyptians had chests with beautiful decorations on them.

A decorated chest found in the annexe shows Tutankhamun in a horse-drawn chariot using a bow. Another chest has a carved scene of the pharaoh sitting down. His wife is at his feet passing him an arrow to shoot at wild birds and fish. Several bows and arrows were in the tomb, as well as a boomerang, which would have been thrown at animals during a hunt.

An unusual small statue shows the pharaoh balancing on a papyrus boat. He is holding a harpoon in his hand, and he is hunting a hippopotamus. Ordinary Ancient Egyptians hunted for food, but these objects show Tutankhamun hunting for sport.

the side of a decorated chest showing Tutankhamun in a horse-drawn chariot

a statue of Tutankhamun hunting

The annexe was also where Carter found four board games. A board with 20 squares was for playing a game called "Thieves". On the other side of the board there are 30 squares for playing a game called "Senet". The playing pieces, which would have been kept in a small drawer, are missing. No clues were left about how to play the games, and no board game we have today is the same as these. However, we do know that the squares represented good or bad luck. Whether you won or lost was down to chance.

Experts believe that adults and children played these games and Tutankhamun may have enjoyed playing them in his lifetime.

playing pieces were kept in the small drawer

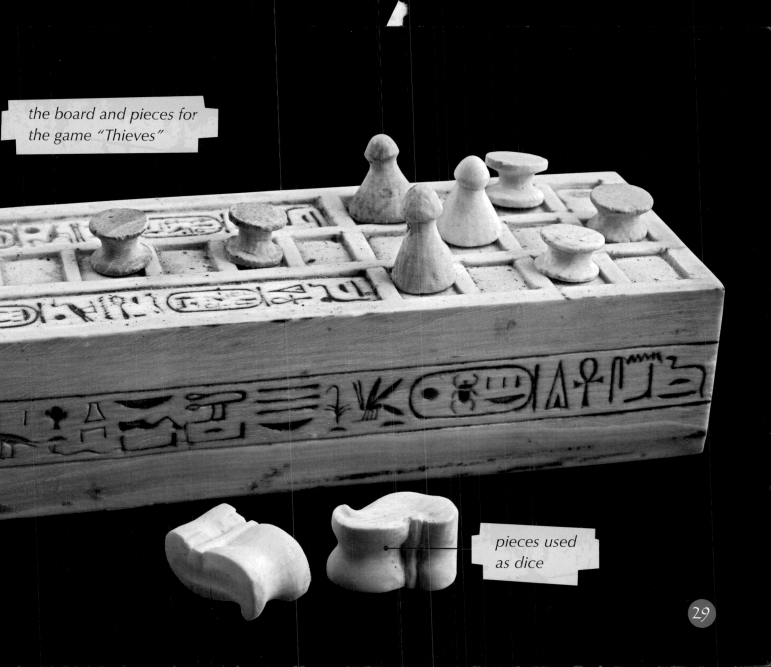

the board and pieces for the game "Thieves"

pieces used as dice

The burial chamber

Outside the door to the burial chamber there were two life-size statues of Tutankhamun himself, guarding the entrance.

This was the only room with painted walls, and it was almost completely filled with a large wooden box called a **shrine**. Inside this shrine was something no one had seen for over 3,000 years – Tutankhamun's stone coffin.

the sealed doorway to Tutankhamun's tomb

statues guarding the entrance to the tomb.

31

Inside the stone coffin were two wooden coffins. Inside those was a third coffin made of solid gold where the mummified body of Tutankhamun lay, wearing a golden mask.

Carter and his team recorded, measured and preserved what they found. They had to be very careful not to damage the mummy, and worked very slowly. It took over 18 months from lifting the lid of the stone coffin to the moment they found the mummified body.

Tutankhamun's golden mask

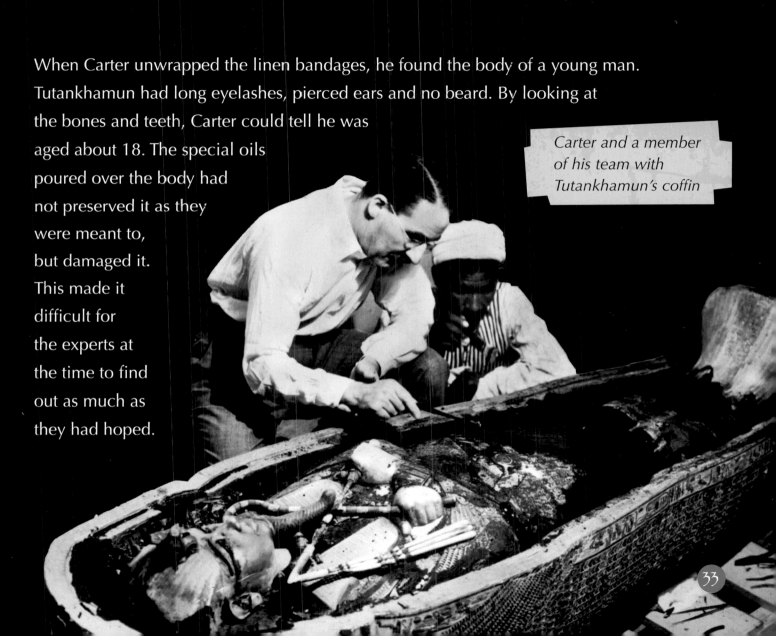

When Carter unwrapped the linen bandages, he found the body of a young man. Tutankhamun had long eyelashes, pierced ears and no beard. By looking at the bones and teeth, Carter could tell he was aged about 18. The special oils poured over the body had not preserved it as they were meant to, but damaged it. This made it difficult for the experts at the time to find out as much as they had hoped.

Carter and a member of his team with Tutankhamun's coffin

33

The treasury

The treasury was guarded by a statue of the god **Anubis**, who had the head of a **jackal**. In this room there was a large gilt chest, model boats and lots of boxes, some labelled "jewels", others "gold rings".

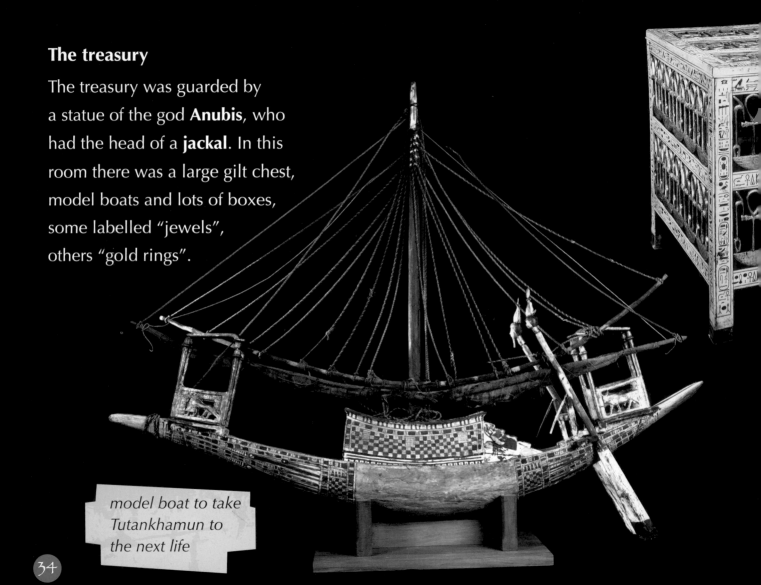

model boat to take Tutankhamun to the next life

More than 400 small wooden figures called shabti were found in the treasury in Tutankhamun's tomb. Some of these figures represent royalty. Others acted as servants for the pharaoh in the next life, and carry farming tools: hoes, picks and baskets.

No ordinary Ancient Egyptian would have had servants like this in their grave. But the wooden figures can tell us what kind of jobs ordinary people did at that time and the importance of farming.

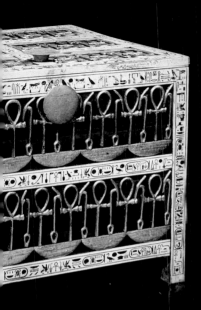

large wooden chest with ivory, gold and silver decoration

The objects this shabti figure is holding show that he is royal. The objects were also used for farming.

35

All the jewellery found in the tomb was made for a pharaoh, not an ordinary Ancient Egyptian. In the treasury Carter found some earrings, necklaces and bracelets, and 143 jewels were found on the mummy itself.

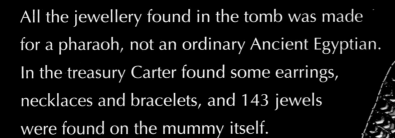

This collar, shaped like a vulture, was found on the mummy.

The collar is made of gold, glass and precious stones.

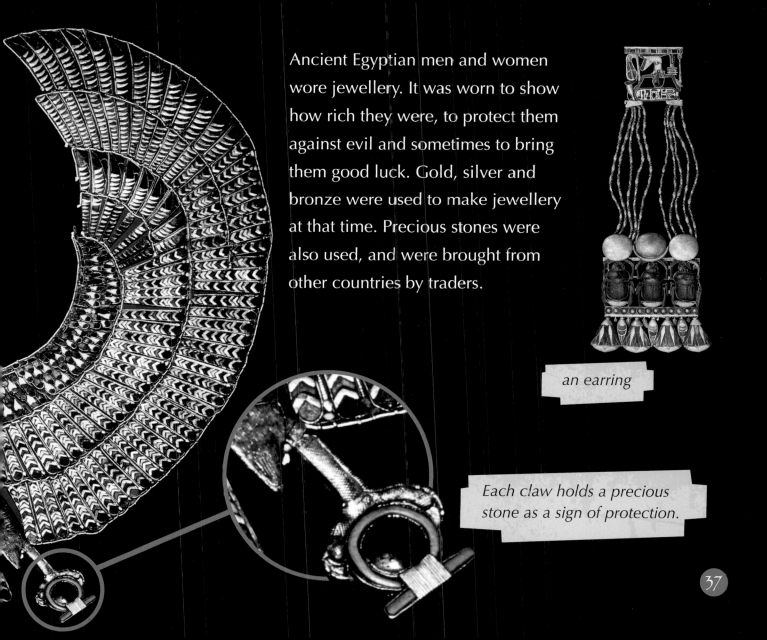

Ancient Egyptian men and women wore jewellery. It was worn to show how rich they were, to protect them against evil and sometimes to bring them good luck. Gold, silver and bronze were used to make jewellery at that time. Precious stones were also used, and were brought from other countries by traders.

an earring

Each claw holds a precious stone as a sign of protection.

Why is Tutankhamun's tomb important?

When Tutankhamun's tomb was first discovered, it was reported in *The Times* newspaper in England. Visitors and journalists from all over the world travelled to the Valley of the Kings to see what had been found. Lord Carnarvon enjoyed the **publicity**, and he held lunch parties in Tutankhamun's tomb. But this made Carter's job more difficult because the tomb was full of people.

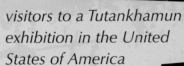

visitors to a Tutankhamun exhibition in the United States of America

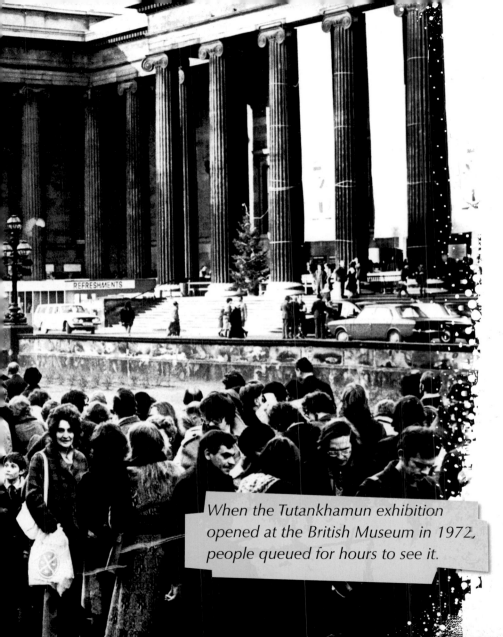

The stone coffin Carter found in the burial chamber, and three of the inner coffins, were left in the tomb in the Valley of the Kings. Everything else found in the tomb was sent to the Cairo Museum, in Egypt. Many years later, the treasures were exhibited around the world. Millions of ordinary people queued up to see the amazing objects, which they had only seen in photographs. It was possible for everyone to learn more about what Egypt was like thousands of years ago.

When the Tutankhamun exhibition opened at the British Museum in 1972, people queued for hours to see it.

What can modern technology tell us?

Today, we can use modern technology like **CT scans** to tell us more
about Tutankhamun. In 2005, a CT scan of Tutankhamun's body showed
that just before he died, he had broken his leg and it had become infected.
Tests revealed that he had a disease called **malaria**. He also had bone disease in
both his feet, so it's likely that Tutankhamun would have walked with a limp.
This explains why there are about 130 walking sticks in his tomb.

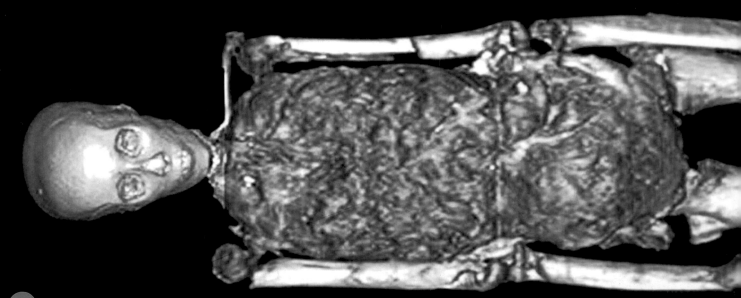

Carter could not have found out information like this because the technology didn't exist in 1922. However, although we now know all these things about Tutankhamun, we still don't know how he died.

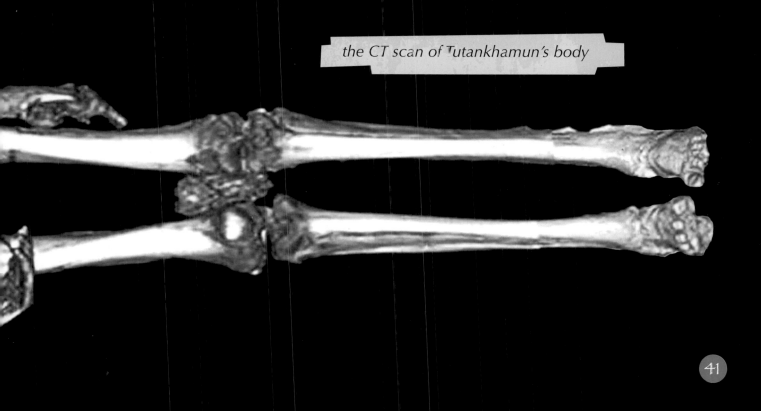

the CT scan of Tutankhamun's body

Is there more to discover?

Before Carter found Tutankhamun's tomb, we didn't know very much about the pharaoh. Now, we know a little more about him: the furniture he owned, the games he may have played, the clothes he wore and the food he ate. We also know what kind of diseases he had. But we still don't know anything more about Tutankhamun's family, how or why he became pharaoh or any other important things that happened to him.

For now, Tutankhamun is a pharaoh better known for his death and tomb than anything he did in his lifetime.

The objects inside Tutankhamun's tomb do, however, tell us more about how Ancient Egyptians lived and worked than we knew before: the skill of the goldsmiths, jewellers, carpenters, weavers, potters, basket makers – as well as the wealth of the country.
We also know more about Ancient Egyptian burial customs. The tomb has revealed more information about life at the time rather than about the pharaoh himself.

There are still hundreds of places in Egypt where archaeologists might find buildings and objects from thousands of years ago. They may well discover something that tells us even more about how Ancient Egyptians lived, worked and died.

tourists in the Valley of the Kings

Glossary

Anubis — the Egyptian god of the dead

archaeologists — people who study the past using objects that have been dug up

BCE — before the common era (the same as BC)

CT scans — electronic pictures of the inside of a body

custom — traditional way of doing something

Egyptology — the study of Ancient Egypt

embalmers — people who preserved dead bodies

gilded — painted with gold

internal organs — inside body parts such as the liver, lungs and kidneys

jackal — a kind of wolf

kingdoms — places ruled by a king or queen

malaria — a serious blood disease passed on by insects called mosquitoes

nobles — important people

papyrus — a tough, paper-like material made from water plants

preserved — treated to stop something from rotting

publicity — telling lots of people about something or someone

pyramids — buildings or 3D shapes with triangular sides that meet at a single point at the top

rosettes — rose-shaped decorations

shrine — a box or room containing an object linked to a dead person or god

skilled — able to do something very well

worshipped — prayed to

Index

The treasures of Tutankhamun's tomb

annexe

antechamber

entrance

46

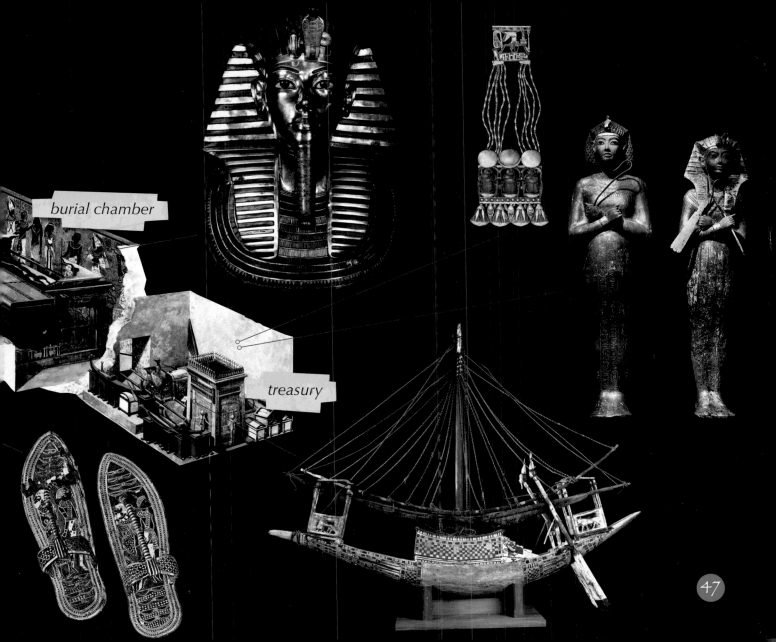

burial chamber

treasury

Ideas for reading

Written by Clare Dowdall BA(Ed), MA(Ed)
Lecturer and Primary Literacy Consultant

Learning objectives: identify and summarise evidence from a text to support a hypothesis; use knowledge of different organisational features of texts to find information effectively; offer reasons and evidence for their views, considering alternative opinions

Curriculum links: History

Interest words: annexe, antechamber, archaeologists, burial chamber, caskets, embalmers, jackal, malaria, papyrus, rosettes, serpent

Resources: paper, pens, ICT

Getting started

This book can be read over two or more reading sessions.

- Find out what the children know about the Ancient Egyptians and explain that this book is about an Ancient Egyptian King called Tutankhamun. List ideas and questions they have about the king inside a mask-shaped outline and save these for later.

- Look closely at the image on the front cover of the book. Discuss what it is showing, and help children to understand that the golden image is a mask, and not Tutankhamun himself. Support children to use powerful adjectives to describe what they can see.

- Read the words *Tutankhamun's Tomb*, and help children to pronounce the name. Notice that the word *Tomb* has a silent consonant, and check that children know what a tomb is.

Reading and responding

- Ask children to read pp2–3 with a partner to find out as much information as possible about the Ancient Egyptians. Question children to help them summarise what they have found out, e.g. *When did they live? What were they called then?* Record any new information around the outside of their mask sheets using a pen in a different colour.

- Draw children's attention to the emboldened words on pp2–3. Model how to look these words up in the glossary to check understanding.

- Ask children to read up to p43 to learn about Tutankhamun, his mummification, and his life. Support children as they read by questioning them and discussing their reading.

Returning to the book

- Using the plan of the tomb on pp46–47, ask children to recount what was found in each room in the tomb, and what the rooms were used for. Support them to justify their ideas by making reference to the appropriate sections of the book.